Happy birthday Daisy,

Learning to meditate has brought me so much joy and calm! So much so ... I wanted to share this with you. No pressure though! Love, Auntie Kate xxx

First published in 2013 by Tharpa Publications.

Tharpa Publications UK Office
Conishead Priory
Ulverston, Cumbria
LA12 9QQ, UK

Tharpa Publications US Office
47 Sweeney Road
Glen Spey
NY 12737, USA

Tharpa Publications is part of the
New Kadampa Tradition – International Kadampa Buddhist Union (NKT-IKBU).
Tharpa has offices around the world and Tharpa books are published in most major languages.

Library of Congress Control Number: 2012953549

British Library Cataloguing in Publication Data
A catalogue record for this book is available from the British Library.

ISBN: 978-1-906665-48-7 – paperback

Set in Candara by Tharpa Publications.

Printed by: CPI Group (UK) Ltd., Croydon, CR0 4YY
Paper supplied from well-managed forests and other controlled sources, and certified in accordance with the rules of the Forest Stewardship Council.

WHAT IS MEDITATION?

GESHE KELSANG GYATSO

Buddhism for Children Level Four

THARPA PUBLICATIONS
UK • US • CANADA
AUSTRALIA • ASIA

What is Meditation?

Tathagata Glorious Light

Tathagata Glorious One without Sorrow • Tathagata Son without Craving

Meditation is an action of mind whose nature is single-pointed concentration and whose function is to make the mind peaceful and calm. We want to be happy all the time, even during our dreams. How can we do this? We can do this through training in meditation because meditation makes our mind become peaceful, and when our mind is peaceful we are happy all the time, even if our external conditions are poor. On the other hand, when our mind is not peaceful we are not happy, even if our external conditions are excellent. We can understand this through our own experience. Since the actual method to make our mind peaceful is training in meditation, we should apply effort to training in meditation. Whenever we meditate, we are performing an action or karma that causes us to

Tathagata Glorious Flower

Tathagata Clearly Knowing through Enjoying Pure Radiance • *Tathagata Clearly Knowing through Enjoying Lotus Radiance*

experience peace of mind in the future. From this we can understand how important meditation practice is.

The objects of our meditation should be those that are meaningful objects, so that through training in meditation we can free ourself permanently from all the sufferings of this life and our countless future lives, and we can attain the supreme happiness of enlightenment, as Buddha showed. This is the best example for us. However, at the beginning we can use our breathing as the object of our meditation and practise breathing meditation, which is quite simple.

How do we practise breathing meditation? First you should relax both physically and mentally, and stop thinking about anything. Then you should gently and naturally inhale and

Tathagata Glorious Wealth

Tathagata Glorious Mindfulness • *Tathagata Glorious Name of Great Renown*

exhale through the nostrils, not through the mouth, and single-pointedly concentrate on the sensation of the breath as it enters and leaves the nostrils. You should remain concentrated on this sensation for as long as possible. If after doing this your mind is still not peaceful you should repeat the above breathing meditation again and again until your mind becomes completely peaceful. Then you should apply effort to remaining continually peaceful day and night. In this way you can make yourself as well as your friends and family happy all the time.

The New Meditation Handbook explains twenty-one objects of meditation, which are meaningful objects. Three of these are essential. These are: renunciation, the supreme good heart, and the profound view of emptiness.

Tathagata King of the Victory Banner, Head of the Powerful Ones

Tathagata Glorious One Complete Subduer   •   Tathagata Great Victor in Battle

Renunciation does not mean that we abandon our friends, families and our human enjoyments. It is an inner realization and not a physical action. To develop renunciation within our mind Buddha advised us, saying, "You should know sufferings." In saying this Buddha is advising us that we should know about the unbearable sufferings that we will experience in our countless future lives, and therefore develop renunciation, the determination to free ourself permanently from these sufferings.

In general, everyone who has physical or mental pain, even animals, understands their own suffering; but when Buddha says "You should know sufferings" he means that we should know the sufferings of our future lives. Through knowing these, we will develop a strong wish to free ourself from them. This practical advice is important for everybody because, if we have

Tathagata Glorious One Complete Subduer Passed Beyond

Tathagata Glorious Array Illuminating All • Tathagata Jewel Lotus Great Subduer

the wish to free ourself from the sufferings of future lives, we will definitely use our present human life for the freedom and happiness of our countless future lives. There is no greater meaning than this.

If we do not have this wish we will waste our precious human life only for the freedom and happiness of this one short life. This would be foolish because our intention and actions would be no different from the intention and actions of animals who are only concerned with this life alone. The great Yogi Milarepa once said to a hunter called Gonpo Dorje:

"Your body is human but your mind is that of an animal.
You, a human being, who possess an animal's mind,
please listen to my song."

Normally we believe that solving the suffering and problems of our present life is most important, and we dedicate our whole life for this purpose. In reality, the duration of the suffering and problems of this life is very short; if we die tomorrow, they will end tomorrow. However, since the duration of the suffering and problems of future lives is endless, the freedom and happiness of our future lives is vastly more important than the freedom and happiness of this one short life. With the words "You should know sufferings" Buddha encourages us to use our present human life to prepare for the freedom and happiness of our countless future lives. Those who do this are truly wise.

In future lives, when we are born as an animal, such as a cow or a fish, we will become the food of other living beings, and we will have to experience many other kinds of animal suffering.

Animals have no freedom, and are used by human beings for food, work and enjoyment. They have no opportunity to improve themselves; even if they hear precious Dharma words it is as meaningless to them as hearing the wind blowing. When we are born as a hungry ghost we will not have even a tiny drop of water to drink; our only water will be our tears. We will have to experience the unbearable sufferings of thirst and hunger for many hundreds of years. When we are born as a hell being in the hot hells, our body will become inseparable from fire and others will be able to distinguish between our body and fire only by hearing our suffering cries. We will have to experience the unbearable torment of our body being burned for millions of years. Like all other phenomena, the hell realms do not exist inherently but exist as mere appearances to mind, like dreams.

Tathagata King of Mount Meru

Seated Firmly on a Jewel and a Lotus

When we are born as a desire realm god we experience great conflict and dissatisfaction. Even if we experience some superficial enjoyment, still our desires grow stronger, and we have even more mental suffering than human beings. When we are born as a demi-god we are always jealous of the gods' glory and because of this we have great mental suffering. Our jealousy is like a thorn piercing our mind, causing us to experience both mental and physical suffering for long periods of time. When we are born as a human being we will have to experience various kinds of human suffering and problems including the sufferings of birth, sickness, ageing and death.

Through studying and understanding the meaning of these teachings, you should make the strong determination thinking, "I must liberate myself permanently from the sufferings of my countless future lives." You should meditate on this determination, which is actual renunciation. You should practise this meditation every day and apply effort to maintain your determination day and night without forgetting it. The actual method to free ourself permanently from the sufferings of our countless future lives is meditation on the profound view of emptiness. Clear and detailed explanations of this meditation can be found in the book *Modern Buddhism.*

The teachings of Buddha presented in this book are principally for children, but anyone who studies and practises these teachings will experience great results.

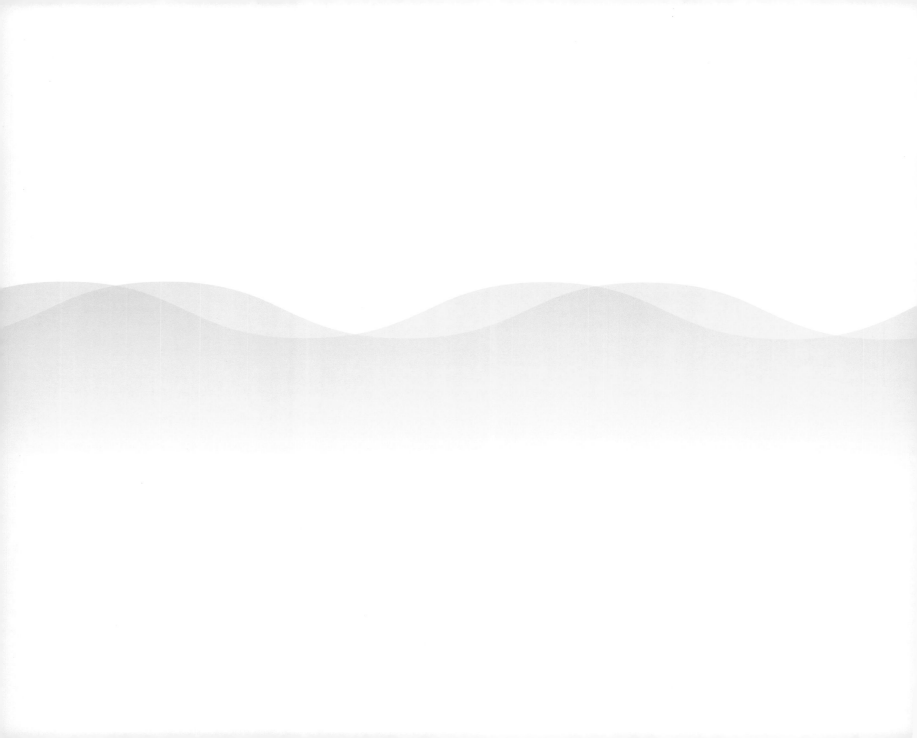

Guidelines for a Simple Breathing Meditation

Guidelines for a Simple Breathing Meditation

Sitting comfortably, check that your back is straight, your eyes partially closed, and your hands are resting gently in your lap. If you wish you can place your right hand in the palm of your left hand with the thumbs raised and gently touching.

Now mentally relax and stop thinking about anything.

Gently and naturally inhale and exhale through the nostrils, not through the mouth, and become aware of the sensation of the breath as it enters and leaves the nostrils.

This sensation is your object of meditation. Try to concentrate on it to the exclusion of everything else.

If any thoughts arise, resist the temptation to follow them and remain focused single-pointedly on the sensation of the breath as it enters and leaves the nostrils.

If you discover that your mind has wandered and is following your thoughts, immediately return it to the sensation of the breath and focus on it single-pointedly.

Repeat this as many times as necessary until the mind settles on the breath.

As your distracting thoughts subside you will experience a sense of inner peace and relaxation. Your mind will feel lucid and spacious and you will feel refreshed.

Stay with this state of mental calm for a while.

Make the determination to try to keep this experience of inner peace and carry it into your daily life.

When you feel ready, relax your concentration and arise from meditation.

You should apply effort to remaining continually peaceful day and night. In this way you can make yourself as well as your friends and family happy all the time.

About the Author

Geshe Kelsang Gyatso, or Geshe-la as he is affectionately known by his students, is a world renowned Buddhist meditation master who has pioneered the introduction of modern Buddhism into contemporary society.

Through his personal example and his public teachings and writings he demonstrates how everyone, whether Buddhist or non-Buddhist, can learn to become wiser and more compassionate by following the advice of Buddha.

Geshe Kelsang is the founder of the International Kadampa Schools Project, which was inaugurated in September 2012 with the opening of the first International Kadampa Primary School in Derbyshire, England.

The *Buddhism for Children* series:

The **Buddhism for Children** series invites children to make a journey of self-discovery and self-improvement to help them realize their full potential.

The purpose is not to convert them to Buddhism but simply to show how everyone, Buddhist or non-Buddhist, can learn something from the teachings of Buddha.

These books address the reader in a mature fashion, using the life and teachings of Buddha as a basis for exploring many of the issues and concerns that confront children today.

Although these books are written principally for children, anyone who wants a clear explanation of the essence of Buddhism and how it applies to modern living will benefit greatly from reading them.

For more books, audio and artwork on Buddhism and Meditation visit: **www.tharpa.com**

Buddhism for Children Level 1
The Story of Angulimala

Buddhism for Children Level 2
The Story of Buddha

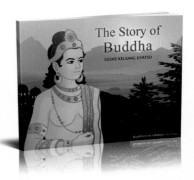

Buddhism for Children Level 3
What is Buddhism?

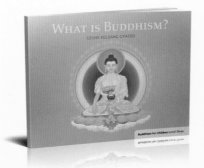

Buddhism for Children Level 4
What is Meditation?

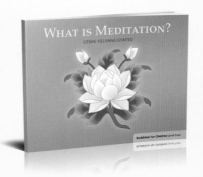